A ROVING EYE

A ROVING EYE
Head to Toe in Egyptian Arabic Expressions

Mona Ateek
Mona Kamel Hassan
Trevor Naylor
Marian Sarofim

Photographs by
Doriana MacMullen

The American University in Cairo Press
Cairo   New York

Mona Ateek has an MA in teaching English as a foreign language and has been teaching in the English Language Institute of the American University in Cairo (AUC) since 1987. Mona Kamel is a senior Arabic language instructor in the Department of Arabic Language Instruction (ALI) at the AUC, and head of Arabic language courses there. Trevor Naylor is the author of Living Normally: Where Life Comes Before Style. He lives normally in Cairo. Marian Sarofim has been teaching English at the AUC since 1972, and is the recipient of the AUC's 2012 Teaching Excellence Award. Doriana MacMullen is a Bulgarian photographer who lives and works in Cairo. Her love of the Egypt and its people is reflected here in what has been her most exciting photography challenge yet.

No relation is intended between the subjects of the pictures in this book and the sayings. Our thanks go to all those who happily took part in the project. We made many friends along the way.

First published in 2014 by
The American University in Cairo Press
113 Sharia Kasr el Aini, Cairo, Egypt
420 Fifth Avenue, New York, NY 10018
www.aucpress.com

Exclusive distribution outside Egypt and North America by I.B.Tauris & Co Ltd., 6 Salem Road, London, W2 4BU

Dar el Kutub No. 10466/14
ISBN 978 977 416 679 2

Dar el Kutub Cataloging-in-Publication Data

Ateek, Mona
A Roving Eye: Head to Toe in Egyptian Arabic Expressions/Mona Ateek.–Cairo: The American University in Cairo Press, 2014.
          p. ill.; cm.
          ISBN 978 977 416 679 2
    1. Proverbs, Arabic
    I. Title
    398.9927

1 2 3 4 5   18 17 16 15 14

Designed by Cherif Abdullah
Printed in China

Preface

Mona Ateek

This book came into being as the result of a mysterious interplay of unexpected and inexplicable forces and currents. Marian, Mona, Trevor, and I are all regular passengers on R9, the bus route that transports faculty, students, and staff from Zamalek to the American University in Cairo campus in New Cairo.

Marian and I, friends and colleagues for many years, teach in the English Language Institute, while Mona teaches Arabic as a foreign language. It was at some undefined point, seated on the bus, that we noticed that there are so many Egyptian expressions related to body parts that keep popping up in people's speech and that colorfully and succinctly express their emotions, or that are critical judgments of a person's character or behavior. We thought it would be an interesting endeavor to collect as many as we could.

And so the list grew from 'head to toe' and when we counted over 150 sayings, we contemplated what our next step should be. We felt that it could be publishable if accompanied by illustrations, but our search for an illustrator was unsuccessful, so we let it rest.

A year passed. Maybe two. Then one day, a tall silver-haired man with sparkling blue eyes got on the bus. As he passed my seat he said, "Hello, Mona." I did not recognize him: it was Trevor, and I had not seen him in more than twenty years! On the journey back we caught up with each other's news. I told him about the list of sayings, and his enthusiastic response and suggestion that photographs be taken instead of illustrations proved to be the missing link.

I'm sure when you read through this compilation, you will find many similar body-part metaphors in your language, whatever it may be. But there will also be those that are culture-specific—very 'Egyptian.' And in Trevor and Doriana's photographs you will find an invitation to come, see, and hear for yourselves. Welcome to Egypt.

Mona Kamel Hassan

Traveling daily to New Cairo and back to Zamalek is tedious for AUC staff, students, and faculty riding the R9 bus. But to look at the bright side: what can I do rather than read, work on the computer, or listen to music? Oh! I can chat with my friends and colleagues, whom I rarely see on the University campus.

Various topics were tackled, among them the abundant amount of idiomatic expressions that Egyptians employ in their conversations to express personal feelings—happiness, sadness, optimism, pessimism—or their attitudes toward others—boasting, criticizing, blaming, advising, etc.

Then there emerged the striking questions raised by Mona Ateek: What is the figurative meaning of these idiomatic expressions? How do students learning Arabic as a foreign language perceive them?

A few weeks after these fruitful conversations, Mona Ateek asked me if I would like to join her and Marian in publishing a book of Egyptian idiomatic expressions. I was excited and immediately expressed my willingness to work with them, particularly as the study of such expressions is one of my areas of interest in the field of sociolinguistics.

I hope that students of Arabic and anyone interested in Egyptian culture will enjoy our work.

Trevor Naylor

Colloquialisms have been part of my life since I first learned to speak. I am from Yorkshire, and there we have a rich, historical range of expressions that most other English speakers fail to understand.

"Where there's muck there's brass" is a good example. I leave you to look that up somewhere later.

This book is about the Arabic terms and phrases that Egyptians use daily, and that refer to parts of the human body or soul. They are full of wit and wisdom, as all proverbs and idioms should be. Homespun philosophy, as we would say in England, where the fascination with our language is the subject of countless books and television or radio shows.

So when the idea of collecting and finding a way to publish such things from Egypt arose with Mona, I was hooked. For me the challenge was how to present these phrases, and Egypt itself, in a visual and modern way for all ages to enjoy and read together as a celebration of people and local life.

The lists that had been prepared by my fellow writers are full of life's good and bad sides, and are packed with emotions and feelings. The photographs had to reflect that, and my great good fortune is to know Doriana and her work. She was on board within seconds of being asked to join the team.

Together she and I set out to take pictures of people in Egypt, all of whom responded to the project enthusiastically, as we hope the images show.

Whether you are an Arabic speaker, or a student, or just love Egypt, this book I hope is for you and anyone else you wish to share the real Egypt with. This is Egyptian Arabic at its best. Enjoy.

Marian Sarofim

As many things in my life, writing this book was not planned. The idea came to us—my good friend, colleague, and bus buddy Mona Ateek and myself—on our tedious bus ride to and from the AUC's new campus. To while the time away, we would chat non-stop, and as we chatted in Arabic we noticed that our conversations were always punctuated with expressions that included parts of the body. So it became a game to see how many of these expressions we could find. Noticing how often our family members, friends, and colleagues also used these expressions, and amazed by the variety and frequency of their usage, we decided to write them down.

Being English-language teachers, we began thinking about how difficult it must be for students of Arabic to understand the usage of these very flowery but very apt and picturesque utterances, and so a book containing a collection of some of these expressions seemed like a good idea. We decided to translate these expressions literally, transliterate them so that learners of Arabic would be able to pronounce them correctly, and explain the usage, but we did not always agree on the usage. It was at this point that Mona Kamel joined us. As she was a teacher of Arabic, and also on the same bus, we would often ask her for her opinions about the correct usage and on how to transliterate certain words.

Seeing us always engaged in lively conversations, another bus buddy, Trevor Naylor, asked Mona Ateek one day what we were always "nattering" about. When he heard of our project he at once offered to take pictures to illustrate our expressions.

So, in a sense the bus ride we always complain about did pay off in the end. Maybe we need to thank bus route R9 for putting us all together and enabling us to produce this book, which we hope will be a useful, fun, educational, pleasing-to-the-eye, thought-provoking window on Egyptian culture, and a wonderful conversation piece, as one can argue endlessly about the meaning and usage of some of these colorful expressions.

Pronunciation Guide

Consonants

2	a glottal stop, as in the middle of *Uh-oh!*
3	the guttural letter *ayn*, pronounced with a constriction far back in the throat, rather like a backward gulp; if you can't manage it, substitute an *a*
7	a 'heavy' *h*, pronounced in the back of the throat, like the sound you might make when you step into an unexpectedly cold shower
D	an 'emphatic' *d*, pronounced with the tongue bunched up in the back of the mouth
S	an 'emphatic' *s*, pronounced with the tongue bunched up in the back of the mouth
T	an 'emphatic' *t*, pronounced with the tongue bunched up in the back of the mouth

g	always 'hard,' as in *get*
sh	as in *ship*
kh	like the *ch* in German *Bach* or Scottish *loch*
gh	pronounced as *kh*, but with the vocal cords vibrating

Doubled consonants indicate a sound held for longer than the single letter: think of the double *k* sound in *bookcase* or the double *m* sound in *homemaker*

Vowels
Doubled vowels indicate long vowel sounds

a	like the *a* in *hat*
aa	like the *ai* in *laird*
å	like the *a* in American *also* or the *o* in British *hot*
åå	like the *ar* in British *hard*
e	like *e* in *get*
ee	like the *ay* in *way*
i	like the *i* in *fish*
ii	like the *ea* in *easy*
o	like the *oa* in *boat*
oo	like the *oa* in *road*
u	like the *u* in *put*
uu	like the *oo* in *food*

وِشّـــك وَلَّا وِشّ الــقَـــمَـــرِ!

wishshik walla wishsh il-2åmår

(Is it your face or the face of the moon?)

Long time no see

بِيِتْخــانِـق مَعَ دِبّــان وِشُّــه

biyitkhaani2 maჳa dibbaan wishshu

(He fights the flies around his face)

He'll pick a fight with anyone

وِشَّـــهـا جِــلْـو عَــلَــيَّـه

wishshaha 7ilw 3alayγa

(Her face is good on me)

She brings me good luck

وِشُّــــــه مْنَـوَّر

wishshu-mnåwwår

(His face is lit up)

He is beaming

حــــاطِـــط وِشُّـــــه فــي الْأَرْض

7ååTiT wishshu fi-l-2årD

(He's putting his face on the ground)

He is ashamed

بَيَّــض وِشّــي

båyyåD wishshi

(He whitened my face)

He made me proud

مِــطَــوّل رَقَــبْــتــي

miTåwwil raꝫabti

(He has lengthened my neck)

He has made me proud

وِشُّـــهُـــم فِـي وِشّ بَـعْـض

wishshuhum fi-wishsh bå3D

(They are face to face)

They are always together

وِشُّـه بَـشُّـوش

wishshu bashuush

(His face is smiling)

He is very pleasant

قَـالْـبَـة وِشَّـك لِـيــه؟

2alba wishshik leeh?

(Why have you turned your face upside-down?)

Why are you scowling?

إيش تِعْـمـل الـمـاشـطَـة فـي الـوِشّ الـعِـكِـر؟

2eesh ti3mil il-måshTå fi-l-wishsh il-3ikir

(What can the beautician do with an unpleasant face?)

You can't make a silk purse out of a sow's ear

وِشُّـــه نَــحْـــس

wishshu na7s

(His face is bad fortune)

He brings me bad luck

وِشَّـهـا يِـقْـطَـع الـخَـمِـيـرة مِ الـبِـيـت

wishshaha yi2Tå3 il-khamiira mi-l-beet

(Her face cuts off the yeast from the house)

She is a sourpuss

سَــوِّد وِشِّــي

sawwid wishshi

(He blackened my face)

He made me look bad

مَـاتِـدِّلُـــوش وِشّ

matiddiluush wishsh

(Don't give him a face)

Don't encourage him

مِـــش طـــايِــق أَشُــوف وِشُّـــه

mish Tååyi2 ashuuf wishshu

(I can't bear to see his face)

I can't stand him

مِـــش قـادِر يِـوَرِّيـــنِـي وِشُّـه

mish 2aadir yiwarrini wishshu

(He can't show me his face)

He is ashamed to face me

مِيـــن الــلِّـــي واخِـــد عَـقْـلِـك؟

miin 2illi waakhid 3a2lik?

(Who took your mind?)

What are you daydreaming about?

ماشِيَة عَلَى حَلّ شَعْرَها

mashya 3ala 7all sha3raha

(She walks on the flow of her hair)

She doesn't care about her reputation

مُخُّـه كِـبِـيـر

mukhkhu-kbiir

(His brain is big)

He is wise and intelligent

15

عَـلَـى راسُـــه رِيـــشَـــة

ʒala råå̊su riisha

(He has a feather on his head)

He thinks he is better than everyone else

مِش عارِف راسُه مِن رِجْلِيه

mish ʒaarif rååsu min rigleeh

(He doesn't know his head from his feet)

He doesn't know whether he's coming or going

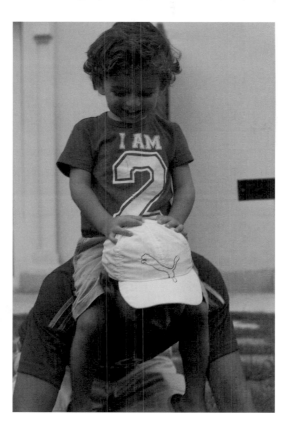

شــا يــلُــه عَــلَــى راسُــه

shaylu ʒala rååsu

(He carries him on his head)

He gives him his all

عـامْلَـة راسْـهـا بـراسِـي

ʒaamla råås-ha b-rååsi

(She makes her head equal to my head)

She acts like she's my equal

مُـخّـه جَـزْمَـة

mukhkhu gazma

(His brain is a shoe)

He is stubborn

خَـبْـطِـتِـيــن فِـي الــرَّاس تِـوْجَـع

khåbTiteen fi-r-råås tiwga3

(Two hits on the head hurt)

It hurts to make the same mistake twice

عَـلَـى راسُـه بَـطْـحَـة

3ala rååsu båT7å

(He has a wound on his head)

He has a chip on his shoulder

اشْـتِري دِمـاغَـك

2ishtiri dimaaghak

(Buy your head)

Don't let it bother you

بَـلاش وَجَـع دِمـاغ

balaash waga3 dimaagh

(Don't give me a headache)

Don't bother me

بِـيْـمَـشِّـي الـلِّـي فِي دِمـاغُـه

biymashshi ziili fi-dimaaghu

(He acts on what's in his head)

He does whatever he wants

مُـخُّـه طَـاقِـق

mukhkhu Tåå2i2

(His brain has cracked)

He doesn't think straight

مُـخُّـه تِـخِـيـن

mukhkhu-tkhiin

(His brain is fat)

He is stupid

طَـيَّـر لِـي بُـرْج مِـن رَاسِـي

Tåyyårli burg min rååsi

(He blew a tower off my head)

He shocked me

23

شَـــعْــر راسِـــي وِقِـــف

sha3r rååsi wi2if

(My hair stood up)

My hair stood on end

خَلِّــي عِـينِـــك فِــي وِسْـط راسِـــك

khalli ʒeenik fi-wiST rååsik

(Keep your eye in the middle of your head)

Be alert

عِيـنْـهـا مَـلْـيـانَـة

ʒenha malyaana

(Her eye is full)

She's content

عِـــيــنُــه زايْـــغَـــة

зeenu zaygha

(His eye wanders)

He has a roving eye

مِـن عِـــيــنِـــي دِي وعِـــيــنِـــي دِي

min 3eeni di wi-3eeni di

(From this eye of mine and this eye of mine)

I'll do whatever you ask

29

عِـين فـي الجَّـنَّـة وعِـيـن فـي النّـار

3een fi-g-ganna wi-3een fi-n-nåår

(An eye in heaven and an eye in hell)

Between a rock and a hard place

عِـينُـه تِـفـلَـق الـحَـجَـر

3eenu tifla2 il-7ågår

(His eye splits the stone)

He is very envious

طَـلَّع عِـيـنِـي

Tållå3 3eeni

(He put out my eye)

He gave me a hard time

دَه بـعِـيـنَـك

da b-3eenak

(That's with your eye)

Absolutely not

نِـزْلِـت مِـن عِيـنُـه

nizlit min 3eenu

(She fell from his eye)

He no longer respects her

حـاحُـطَّـهـا فِـي عِيـنِـي

7a7uTTåhå fi-3eeni

(I will put her in my eye)

I will take good care of her

مِـش مـالِـي عِيـنْـهـا

mish maali 3enha

(He doesn't fill her eye)

She doesn't think he's good enough for her

إِلْـعِيـن مـا تِـعْلاش عَـن الـحـاجِـب

il-3een mati3laash 3an il-7a3gib

(The eye does not rise above the brow)

Know your place

عِـينِـي فِـي عِـينَـك

ʒeeni fi-ʒeenak

(My eye in your eye)

Tell me the truth

حاشِر مَنـاخِيــرُه في كُلّ حـاجَـة

7aashir manakhiiru fi-kull 7aaga

(He sticks his nose into everything)

He's nosy

عَامِـل وِدن مِن طـيـن ووِدن مِن عَجْـيـن

3aamil widn min Tiin wi-widn min 3agiin

(He's making one ear of mud and one of clay)

He doesn't want to listen

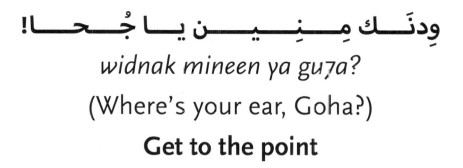

وِدنَــك مِــنِــيــن يـا جُـحـا!

widnak mineen ya gu7a?

(Where's your ear, Goha?)

Get to the point

رامــــي وِدنُـــــه

raami widnu

(He's throwing his ear)

He's eavesdropping

حاطَّـة إيدِك عَـلَـى خَـدِّك لِـيـه؟

7åTTå 2iidik zala khaddik leeh?

(Why do you have your hand on your cheek?)

Why do you look so sad?

مِــن بُــقَّــك لِــبــاب الــسَّــمــا

min bu22ak li-baab is-sama

(From your mouth to the gate of heaven)

May what you say come true

بُقَّهـا مـا يِتْبَلِّش فِــيـه فُولَــة

bu22aha mayitballish fiih fuula

(A bean doesn't get wet in her mouth)

She can't keep a secret

فــاشِــخ بُـقُّــه مِ الْـوِدْن دِي لِلْـوِدْن دِي

faashikh buƶƶu mi-l-widn di li-l-widn di

(He's stretching his mouth from
this ear to that ear)

He's grinning from ear to ear

خَـلِّـي كَـلامِـي حَـلَـقَـة في وِدْنَـك

khalli kalaami 7ala2a fi-widnak

(Make my words an earring in your ear)

Remember my advice

لَـمّـا تـشُـوف حَـلَـمِـة وِدْنَك

lamma tshuuf 7alamit widnak

(When you see your earlobe)

Pigs might fly

نـايْـمَـة عـلـى وِدانْـهـا

nayma 3ala widanha

(She is sleeping on her ears)

She has no idea what's going on

وِدنُـه بِـتِـسـمـع دَبِّـة الـنَّـمـلـة

widnu bitisma3 dabbit in-namla

(His ear hears the ant's footstep)

He doesn't miss a thing

لِـــــسَانُــهــا زَيّ الـفَــرْقِــلَّــة

lisanha zayy il-far2illa

(Her tongue is like a whip)

She has a sharp tongue

لِـــــسَانُـــه مِـــتْـبَـــرِّي مِـــنُّـــه

lisaanu mitbarri minnu

(His tongue is ashamed of him)

He says embarrassing things

مَـــسْـحُــوب مِـــن لِـــسَانُـــه

mas7uub min lisaanu

(He was dragged [from the womb] by his tongue)

He has a ready answer for everything

قَـــطْـع لِـــسَانُـــه

2åT3 lisaanu

(Cut off his tongue)

How dare he say that!

لِـــــسَـــانُـه بِــيْـنَـقَّـط عَــسَـل

lisaanu biynå22åT ʒasal

(His tongue drips honey)

He says the sweetest things

سِيــرِتْـهـا بَقِـت عَلَــى كُلّ لِـسان

sirit-ha ba2it 3ala kull lisaan

(Her name is on every tongue)

Everyone is talking about her

سِنّ سـنـانَـك

sinn snaanak

(Sharpen your teeth)

Gird your loins

لِـمِّ لِـسـانَـك

limm lisaanak

(Collect your tongue)

Watch your tongue

47

خَــد عَــلَــى قَــفـاه

khad 3ala 2afaah

(He took it on the back of his neck)

He was taught a good lesson

قَــفـاه بــيـقـمَّــر عِــش

2afaah biy2åmmår 3eesh

(The back of his neck bakes bread)

He's idle

مـخـتُــوم عـلــى قَــفـاه

makhtuum 3ala 2afaah

(He's branded on the back of his neck)

He's naive

رَقـبْـتـي سـدّادة

ra2abti saddaada

(My neck is a support)

You can count on me

خـــلَّـــى رَقَـــبْـــتـــي قَـــدّ الـــسِّـــمـــسِـــمـــة

khalla ra2abti 2add is-simsima

(He made my neck as small as a sesame seed)

He embarrassed me

عـــامِـــل زَيّ الـــلُّـــقْـــمَـــة فِـــي الـــزُّور

3aamil zayy il-lu2ma fi-z-zcor

(He's like a piece of bread stuck in the throat)

He's a pain in the neck

مـــابْـــتِـــنْـــزِلِّـــيـــش مِـــن زُور

mabtinzilliish min zoor

(She doesn't go down my throat)

I can't bear her

حِـــلّ عَـــن قَـــفـــايـــا

7ill 3an 2afaaya

(Get away from the back of my neck)

Get lost

ماسْكُـه مِـن رَقَـبْـتُـه

masku min raӡabtu

(I'm holding him by his neck)

I have him under my thumb

وَرِّيـنِي عَـرْض كِــتـافَـك

warriini 3årD kitaafak

(Show me the width of your shoulders)

Go away

شــايِـل الـشِّـرْكَـة عَـلَـى كِـتـافُـه

shayil ish-shirka 3ala kitaafu

(He carries the company on his shoulders)

He runs the business single-handed

إيــدُه مـاشْـــكَـة

2iidu maska

(His hand is tight)

He is tight-fisted

53

إيـدِي بـإيـدْهـا

ʒiidi bi-ʒid-ha

(My hand in her hand)

I help her with everything

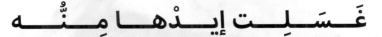

غَــسَــلِــت إيـدْهـا مِنُّـه

ghasalit 2id-ha minnu

(She washed her hand from him)

She washed her hands of him

إيــد عَــلَـى إيــد تِــســاعِـــد

2iid 3ala 2iid tisaa3id

(A hand on a hand helps)

People should help each other

إِيـدِي عَـلَـى كِـتْـفَـك

ʒiidi ʒala kitfak

(My hand on your shoulder)

You lead, I'll follow

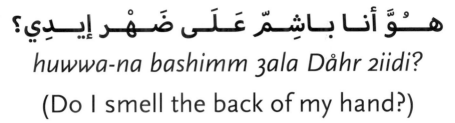

هُوَّ أنـا بـاشِمّ عَـلَى ضَـهْـر إيـدِي؟

huwwa-na bashimm ʒala Dåhr 2iidi?

(Do I smell the back of my hand?)

How would I know?

لازِمِ تِـبُـوس إِيـدَك وِشّ وِضَـهْـر

laazim tibuus 2iidak wishsh u-Dåhr

(You must kiss your hand front and back)

Be grateful for what God gave you

شــاِيـْلـها عَـلَـى كِـفُـوف الرَّاحَـة

shaayilha ʒala kifuuf ir-råå7a

(He's carrying her on the palms of comfort)

He takes good care of her

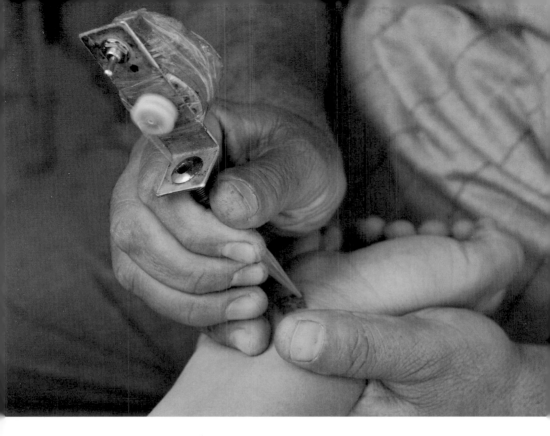

صَـوابْـعَـك مِـش زَيّ بَـعْـضَـهـا

Såwååb3ak mish zayy bå3Dåha

(Your fingers are not all alike)

No two things are exactly the same

63

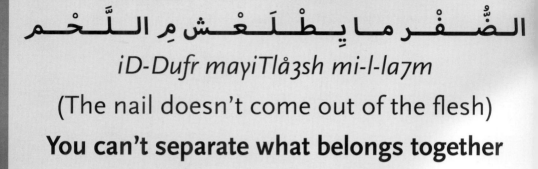

الـضُّـفُـر مـا يـطْـلَـعْـش مِ الـلَّـحْـم

iD-Dufr mayiTlå3sh mi-l-la7m

(The nail doesn't come out of the flesh)

You can't separate what belongs together

حــاطِــط إيـــدُه فِـي مَــيَّــة بازْدَة

7ååTiT 2iidu fi måyyå barda

(He has his hand in cold water)

He is indifferent

اللِّـي إيـدُه فِـي الْـمَـيَّـة مِـش زَيّ اللِّـي إيـدُه فِـي الـنّار

2illi 2iidu fi-l-måyyå mish zayy 2illi 2iidu fi-n-nåår

(He whose hand is in the water is not like him
whose hand is in the fire)

He who is not suffering doesn't feel the suffering of others

مـاسِـكِـنـي مـن الإيـد الـلِّـي بِـتِـوْجَـعْـنِـي

masikni min il-2iid 2illi bitiwga3ni

(He has me by the hand that hurts)

He knows my weak points

مــالِــي إيـــدُه

maali 2iidu

(He has filled his hand)

He is confident

عَضّ الإيــد اللّــي اتْـمَـدِّت لـُه

3åDD il-2iid 2illi itmadditlu

(He bit the hand that was held out to him)

He is ungrateful

خِـفّ إيـدَك

khiff 2iidak

(Make your hand light)

Be quick about it

سَـلَـت إيـدُه مـن الـمَـوْضُـوع

salat 2iidu min il-mawduu3

(He pulled his hand from the subject)

He is no longer involved in the matter

مـاحَـدِّش ضَـرَبَـك عَـلَـى إيـدَك

ma7addish Dåråbak 3ala 2iidak

(No one hit you on your hand)

It's your own fault

عَـلَـى قَـلْـبِـي زَيّ الْـعَـسَـل

3ala 2albi zayy il-3asal

(He is like honey on my heart)

I adore him

حاطِط فِي بَطْنُه بَطِّيخَة صِيفِي

7ååTiT fi-båTnu båTTikha Seefi

(He's put a summer watermelon in his stomach)

He's confident

قَـلْـبِـي مَـعـاك

2albi maჳaak

(My heart is with you)

I feel for you

70

عَـلَـى قَـلْـبُـه مَراوِح

3ala 2albu mårååwi7

(He has fans on his heart)

He plays it cool

تِـقِــيــل عَــلَــى قَــلْــبِــي

ti2iil 3ala 2albi

(He is heavy on my heart)

I don't like him

قَــلْبَــك أبــيَــض

2albak 2åbyåd

(Your heart is white)

You are forgiving

قَــلْبَــهــا حَــجَــر

2albaha 7ågår

(Her heart is stone)

She is cruel and unfeeling

قَــلْبَــهــا مِــش عَــلِــيــك

2albaha mish 3aleek

(Her heart is not on you)

She doesn't have your interest at heart

جَـمِّـد قَـلْـبَـك

gammid 2albak

(Harden your heart)

Be brave

قَـلْـبُـه مَـيِّـت

2albu mayyit

(His heart is dead)

He is cold-hearted

قَـلْـبُـه كِـبِـيـر

2albu-kbiir

(His heart is big)

He is big-hearted

مـاسِـك قَـلْـبُـه بِـإيـدُه

maasik 2albu bi-2iidu

(He's holding his heart in his hand)

He's worried

لـُه ضَـهْـر

luh Dåhr

(He has a back)

He has connections

أفْـدِيــك بِـرُوحِـي

2afdiik bi-roo7i

(I will sacrifice my soul for you)

I will do anything to defend you

دَمَّهـا سِـمّ

dammaha simm

(Her blood is poison)

She is unpleasant

دَفَـع دَمّ قَـلْـبُـه

dafa3 damm 2albu

(He paid the blood of his heart)

He paid a very high price

فَـوَّر دَمِّـي

fåwwår dammi

(He made my blood boil)

He made my blood boil

دَمُّـه نِـشِـف

dammu nishif

(His blood dried up)

He was frightened

حَـــسَـــيِّـــح دَمُّـــه

7asayya7 dammu

(I will make his blood flow)

I'll beat the living daylights out of him

دَمُّـــه خَـــفِـــيـــف

dammu khafiif

(His blood is light)

He has a good sense of humor

دَمُّـــه تِـــقِـــيـــل

dammu-t2iil

(His blood is heavy)

He's charmless

مـــاعَـــنْـــدُوش دَمّ

ma3anduush damm

(He has no blood)

He doesn't care about other people's feelings

مِــن لَــحْــمِــي وِدَمِّــي

min la7mi wi-dammi

(He's of my flesh and blood)

I can't hurt him, he's family

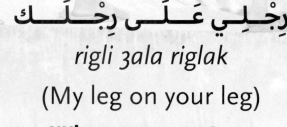

رِجْـلِي عَـلَـى رِجْـلَـك

rigli ʒala riglak

(My leg on your leg)

Where you go I go

رِجْـلِـيـه مِش شايْـلاه

rigleeh mish shaylaah

(His legs don't carry him)

He is very weak

إِيــدي وِرِجْــلي

2iidi wi-rigli

(He's my hand and foot)

He's very useful to me

رِزْقُـــه فِـي رِجْـلِـيـه

riz2u fi-rigleeh

(His livelihood is in his legs)

He is lucky wherever he goes

عَـلَـى رِجْـلُـه نَـقْـش الْـجِـنَّـة

3ala riglu na2sh il-7inna

(He has a henna tattoo on his leg)

He is lazy

جـابت رِجْـلُـه

gaabit riglu

(She brought his leg)

She got him involved in trouble

بـاجُـرّ رِجْـلَـهـا

bagurr riglaha

(I'm pulling her leg)

I'm getting her involved

رِجْلِــيــه بِـتْخَبَّـط فِـي بَـعْـضَـهـا

rigleeh bitkhåbbåT fi-bå3Dåha

(His legs knock together)

He's terrified

وِقِـــف عَـــلَـى رِجْـلِـــيــه

wi2if 3ala rigleeh

(He stood on his legs)

He's back on his feet

قَـطَـع رِجْـلُـه مِـن هِـنــا

2åTå3 riglu min hina

(He cut off his leg from here)

He no longer comes here

بِـيْـقَـدِّم رِجْـل وِيْـأَخَّـر رِجْـل

biy2addim rigl wi-yi2åkhkhår rigl

(He puts one leg forward and one leg back)

He's hesitant

85

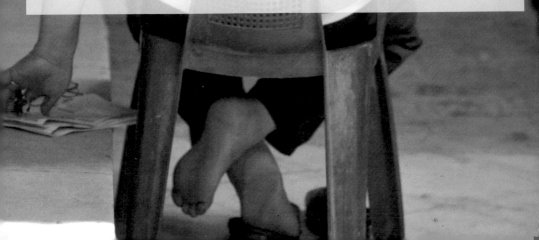

دِي فَرْكِةْ كَعْب

di farkit ka3b

(It's the distance of a heel)

It's very close by